Rousseau / Dufy

Text and Notes by
ALFRED WERNER
Contributing Editor,
ARTS MAGAZINE

TUDOR PUBLISHING COMPANY
New York

Raoul Dufy

To Judith

All rights reserved

TUDOR PUBLISHING COMPANY

New York, 1970

Library of Congress Catalog Card Number: 71–122435

SBN 8148–0335–0

Printed in Japan

HENRI ROUSSEAU

By a sheer miracle, Henri-Julien-Félix Rousseau, the first son of Julien Rousseau and his wife Eléonore, did not become a tinsmith, as his father and grandfather had done. For in the small city of Laval, in northwestern France, the world never changed. Neither his three older sisters nor his younger brothers broke the pattern. As a provincial artisan, he would have married a girl from the same quarter, raised a family and lived a simple life that was as devoid of triumphs and intimations of grandeur as it was of anguish.

Fate willed otherwise. On September 4, 1910, when the body of the sixty-six-year-old Henri Rousseau was buried in a pauper's grave, the small funeral procession included the famous painter Paul Signac. For the dead man had been a member of the Société des Artistes Indépendants of which Signac was founder and president. Most of those who had appreciated the "gentle Rousseau," *le Douanier* (customs inspector), were still on vacation. But after learning of his death, two friends purchased a plot and erected a monument to pay belated homage to the self-taught artist. On the tombstone, the sculptor Constantin Brancusi chiseled an epitaph contributed by the poet Guillaume Apollinaire. It reads, in part:

> *Let our baggage through customs at heaven's gate duty-free*
> *We bring you brushes paints canvases.*
> *So you can devote your sacred leisure in the real light*
> *To painting just as you drew my portrait*
> *The face of the stars*

In 1910, Rousseau was understood only by a score of rather young fellow artists (among them Pablo Picasso) and writers (among them the above-mentioned Apollinaire). Today, six decades later, the very canvases that were jeered at when first exhibited at the Salon des Indépendants are the prized possessions of museums in France, England, Russia, Switzerland and the United States. The same city of Laval which had refused to buy from him for a modest sum *The Sleeping Gypsy* (Plate 18, now in the Museum of Modern Art, New York), finally welcomed the remains of her celebrated son, thanks to Delaunay and others, and interred them in the garden of the local museum. Scores of books and hundreds of articles in French, German, English, Italian and even Japanese seek to penetrate *le mystère Rousseau*—the same Rousseau who had once been dismissed as a dolt.

His is the familiar story of the unrecognized genius, but with a peculiar twist—for Rousseau was the first "outsider" to enter the annals of art, the first "naïve" painter to gain international fame. Gauguin, to be sure, had been a "Sunday painter" before giving up his job as a stockbroker and devoting himself fully to the pursuit of art. But he was a sophisticated Parisian with wide experience, who had Camille Pissarro for a mentor; whereas every biographical detail concerning Rousseau indicates that he was an utter *ingénu,* with only the most rudimentary education. His was a special case, impossible to compare with anyone else's.

When the American painter Max Weber said to him, "Your pictures seem to me as beautiful as those of Giotto," the little old man asked in puzzlement, "Who was Giotto?" Yet Weber's judgment does not amaze us, nor does the defense of Rousseau's work by Henri Toulouse-Lautrec, when the hanging committee of the Indépendants sought to expel their mirth-provoking colleague, whose participation in their jury-free group exhibitions had become an embarrassment. Lautrec clearly sensed the spark of genius in this simple man who combined features of Don Quixote, Prince Mishkin and Kaspar Hauser. In a similar fashion, Camille Pissarro, shown samples of Rousseau's work, instead of laughing as expected, warmly praised them. He was stirred by the qualities of this untutored petit-bourgeois: the direct approach, the inherent sense of design and the virility of color. Edgar Degas, as well, noted Rousseau's feeling for rhythm and color relationships; his talent for simplification; the anachronistic, yet exciting vision of a child freshly discovering the world. "Why shouldn't that be the painter of the future?" Degas asked a group of friends, pointing to a picture by Rousseau.

Degas, it will be remembered, was cautious in his critical pronouncements. His praise gains in weight when one considers the social and intellectual gap

6

between this most cultured aristocrat and the good Rousseau, whose education had never gone beyond the fundamentals, who had never attended an art school, and who had but the vaguest idea of perspective and modeling. Maurice Vlaminck's background was closer to Rousseau's; still, it is significant that he, who more often than not used violent language against his fellow artists, praised the "so rare gift of his [Rousseau's] creation" and voiced "surprise at finding immediately in this *bonhomme* what we seek through knowledge."

Only in the light of appraisals like these—to which could be added appreciations by the painter André Derain, the critics Arsène Alexandre and Elie Faure, the dealer Wilhelm Uhde, and many others—does Rousseau's remark to young Picasso sound less absurd than at first hearing: "We are the two greatest painters of this era, you in Egyptian style, I in modern style. . . ."

Picasso's pre-Cubist squat nudes were, of course, suggested by late Iberian sculpture rather than by Egyptian art; and Rousseau himself was as modern as the old provincial city of Laval where he was born or the petit-bourgeois Plaisance quarter in Paris where he settled and which he left only for strolls through the Jardin des Plantes and the rural suburbs, or to trundle his canvases in a small handcart to the Salon des Indépendants. Nevertheless, Rousseau was one of the truly great painters of his era in that he helped, although unwittingly, to initiate the new anti-Renaissance movement in art. His admirer, Degas, and most of the painters grouped together under the term "Impressionists," still belonged to the Renaissance tradition. Rousseau, only a little younger than they, prepared the way for the elementary forms of Jean Arp, the poetic improvisations of Paul Klee, the anti-intellectualism of Joan Miró, the raw and deliberately uncivilized *art brut* of Jean Dubuffet, and all those twentieth-century creators who emulate the visions of children, aborigines and psychotics.

Yet Rousseau, too poor to enroll in an art school, was entirely self-taught. He claims to have gotten "some advice" from a rather obscure painter, Félix Clément, and from Léon Gérôme, a celebrated academician whose style, as one scholar put it, "combined the clear linearism of his neoclassic training with a sense of sentimentality and, at times, eroticism in the literary interpretation of subject matter." Gérôme's influence can be found in Rousseau's insistence upon finished painting, and in what Gérôme called "luminous and alluring color." But Gérôme's work is self-conscious and often stilted; it lacks all the freshness, the folk-style directness and immediacy of the best of Rousseau's pictures.

7

But what is the real secret of Rousseau's success, and, by the same token, of Gérôme's failure? Those who have sought a convincing answer have often pointed to the dictum of the poet Charles Baudelaire, according to whom genius was but "childhood recovered." There is, indeed, the stunning phenomenon of the child's fantasy and freedom to create that vanishes (alas!) at the approach of adolescence. Pedagogues have found that children, left to their own resources, express themselves in a refreshingly original manner, blending poetic intuition with untrammeled observation. When adult concepts are forced upon them, their artistic output becomes unnatural and unoriginal.

But nature does not give even the most gifted children the strength and skill to conceive and bring forth a masterwork like *The Sleeping Gypsy*. What excited advanced artists and critics six decades ago, and what continues to fascinate sensitive people to this day, is the phenomenon of a man whose imagination did not run dry after he left the sheltered realm of childhood for the merciless world of adults. Rousseau never grew up either intellectually or emotionally; his literary efforts at drama might have come from the pen of a ten-year-old, and he was a failure as a husband and father.

Ironically, Rousseau was, on the whole, unaware of his peculiar status as an artist. When the hanging committee of the Indépendants discussed the possible expulsion of an unnamed embarrassing member, Rousseau was all in favor of this action. It did not occur to this innocent soul that it was he who was being discussed. He had joined the avant-garde Indépendants only after the official Salon to which he had aspired had refused his works; and in an autobiographical sketch submitted in 1895 for a book on contemporary painters, he blithely described himself as "one of the best realist [sic!] artists."

He aspired to nothing higher than to paint with a miraculously polished technique and in the style of Gérôme, or, better still, in that of the arch-academician Adolphe-William Bouguereau, whose death in 1905 distressed him deeply. As one biographer wrote, Rousseau was a primitive in performance rather than in intention. If, in his formative years, he had been given the opportunity to attend the Ecole des Beaux-Arts, he might have become a minor Bouguereau or Gérôme. These Beaux-Arts teachers, who considered it their mission to foster polished, mechanical craftsmanship rather than originality, would have encouraged Rousseau's only conspicuous bourgeois trait, his unfortunate yearning for the respectability he never achieved. It was one of the contradictions in his character that while he led a most unorthodox, bohemian life, he always chose for his self-portraits the most formal attire. Nor did he forget to paint in the little violet rosette he always wore in his lapel—a minor decoration he received from the government for his contribution to a local adult-education project.

Only a Gustave Moreau might have given him the guidance proper to his native talent. Had he been helped by this wise and progressive teacher of Henri Matisse and Georges Rouault, Rousseau would not have had to waste years in trying to acquire the fundamentals of technique. Moreau, who so strongly insisted on individualism, might have enabled Rousseau to become a modern Piero di Cosimo, a bird of poetry soaring to the sun with fully developed wings.

As it was, Rousseau, lacking an aesthetics of his own, had only one desire, and a very simple one: to reproduce what he saw, precisely and exactly as he saw it. When painting a portrait, he used the handle of his brush, as a tailor would use a tape, to measure a client. To make sure he had gotten the right flesh tone, he held a brush dipped in pink up to the sitter's face.

Rousseau's leaf-by-leaf rendering of a tree is, at first sight, reminiscent of the art of children. Unlike a child, however, the artist had the gift of perceiving the gestalt of the object and could reassemble and fuse these hundreds of elements into a unity. In *Forest of Vincennes* (22), he no doubt recorded what he saw as carefully and literally as possible. Yet the composition is firmly held together by the intertwined branches of the young trees, drawn so "unrealistically" (unintentionally!) that they seem like dancers in a surrealist ballet.

Every Rousseau canvas has elements that raise it high above child, folk, or amateur art. Whenever he painted flowers (16, 25 and 43), he scrupulously arranged the blossoms in a vase, then rendered each leaf and petal with minute care. But though he saw each flower singly, he never lost the idea of the bouquet. There is music in these flower paintings, and drama. Rousseau is known to have been worse than a mediocre violinist, and his dramatic writings are plainly silly; but he knew how to orchestrate flowers into striking color harmonies, and to accentuate their beauty by keeping table tops and vases austere and subdued.

The picture of the novelist Pierre Loti (30), painted after a newspaper sketch, has a tinge of naïveté about it; it is neither a psychological study nor a

9

good likeness. Nevertheless, the eyes burn with a passionate intensity, as they do in all of Rousseau's portraits, revealing not so much the sitter as the strange man who painted the canvas. The painter, who looked like any pensioned official and solid family man (see his self-portrait, Plate 1), harbored inside him a fire that would have destroyed him had it not found its outlet in art.

With the same intensity, the lions and tigers in his jungle paintings (5, 28) stare at us out of big, round eyes. These wild beasts are painted after sketches made in the Paris Zoo, while the exotic flora came from the botanical gardens (both located in the Jardin des Plantes). For Rousseau probably never set foot outside France, and the story that as a young man he spent time in Mexican jungles as a member of a French expeditionary corps is no longer accepted. But, as always, imagination got the better of him, resulting in the creation of large tapestries in which every detail is linked to every other with the mad logic of a dream. In one early canvas (5), the imaginary jungle is in upheaval; a storm tosses the tall grasses and the branches of the trees through which a terror-stricken tiger skulks. In an untouched primordial landscape much too ordered to be real (31), the animals peacefully pose for the artist. Many of the jungle scenes, however, depict lions and tigers attacking natives or other animals (28 and 35). To us, these scenes are no more frightening than fairy tales, but for the poet Rousseau everything was real. When he painted a subject of this sort, he frightened himself so much that he had to run to the window for fresh air.

Undoubtedly, the "realist" Rousseau preserved a gift which most people lose along with their childhood: the ability not only to dream, but also to fix visions permanently in color and line. Years after his death, there was much talk in artistic circles about the "omnipotence of the dream," of "hand-painted dream photographs." But whereas the Surrealists who used these phrases were cerebral sophisticates, there is nothing contrived or studied about the work of Rousseau, who apparently did little more than painstakingly transfer his daydreams to canvas. None of the Surrealists produced a picture as aesthetically convincing as *The Sleeping Gypsy* (18), in which a dark-skinned woman sleeps in the desert, watched by a mesmerized lion. First exhibited in 1897, it is one of the most astonishing pictures of the century and is now adored by children, fascinating to Freudian analysts because it lends itself to rich interpretation, and revered by artists. Next to it in New York's Museum of Modern Art hangs Rousseau's last great work, *The Dream* (detail on jacket). This canvas of

1910 superbly summarizes all the elements in Rousseau's jungle series: the tropical flowers and fruits, stylized, and drawn many times their original size; the wild beasts and strange birds in the mass of dark and dense verdure; the white moon in the light sky; and in the center two eerie figures—a nude woman on a red couch and a dark snake charmer piping a melody that can almost be heard.

Something must be said to separate *le Douanier* sharply from the ambitious, nonprofessional "lonely crowd" that has found in pigment and brush a means to fatten an ego. Art was not Rousseau's hobby, but the essence of his life. Had he, like Cézanne, been the son of a banker rather than of a tinsmith, Rousseau might have taken up painting earnestly in his youth, never to do anything else. In his autobiographical sketch, he explained that it was only his parents' poverty that obliged him to follow at first another career (he began as a clerk to a local attorney, and later for many years was a toll collector) than that to which his artistic taste called him. He speaks of his "many mortifications," of his "hard experiences," referring, significantly, not to his financial difficulties, but to his utter lack of training.

While he was simple in many ways, he was clever enough to know that the perfection he sought could be acquired only through "obstinate toil." At any rate, from 1885—and especially from 1893, when he retired from the customs service on a tiny and inadequate pension—to his death in 1910, he devoted himself to art with an unsurpassed zeal. The Maîtres Populaires de la Réalité— as Rousseau and, after him, Louis Vivin, André Bauchant, and the still-living Camille Bombois were called to distinguish them from the lower status of Peintres du Dimanche ("Sunday painters")—were not hobbyists relaxing after hours of real work, but geniuses denied a formal education and struggling mightily against a thousand odds to reach their goal.

But perhaps the last words on Rousseau might be spoken here by two younger colleagues, academically trained artists who knew and loved him. First, Robert Delaunay (quoted by Jean Bouret):

"One feels his [Rousseau's] patience throughout the execution of the picture, every inch of the canvas is painted decisively the very first time: there is no retouching, every movement of his hand counts in the completeness of his work, which his exalted visions present to us, guiding it from start to finish. Nothing will change, so to speak, in the course of the execution from the preliminary indications which he has lightly sketched out on the white canvas. He will only add improving, more expressive details which he discovers in the course of execution, but which are subservient to the general direction of his vision; this is ever present in its full, complete intensity, it is unalterable and does not gainsay the total effect he saw when he traced the first lines of the composition. There are a multitude of broken colors, a mixture of greys and an utmost variety subjected to the constant control of his will, his sensibility and the needs of the subject represented."

The second statement is by an American. In an *Art News* article, the painter Max Weber, who, when still a student in Paris, knew "that angel Rousseau," recalled: "To enter his studio was like going into a fresh vineyard from a murky world. He seemed a pure, almost saintly man, full of love and joyous at the sight of the world. He was not an 'amateur'; painting was his central expression, his whole life."

Rich, D. C., *Henri Rousseau* (New York, 1942)
Werner, A., *Henri Rousseau* (New York, 1953)
Bouret, J., *Henri Rousseau* (Greenwich, Conn., 1961)
Vallier, D., *Henri Rousseau* (New York, 1962)

RAOUL DUFY

The time has come for a new look at Raoul Dufy, one of the great modern French painters, printmakers and designers. For some years after his death, he was either neglected entirely or dismissed as a witty illustrator or a virtuoso decorator with a pleasant flair for color. Seemingly, he no longer fitted into an art world where abstraction was proclaimed the sole deity. Moreover, in his years of fame much damage was done to his reputation by imitation Dufys that inconspicuously bore the names of petty plagiarizers or, worse still, were outright fakes with prominent forged "Dufy" signatures.

It has taken the world almost two decades to learn to separate, once and for all, his true poetry from the purple prose of pseudo-Dufys. Now a new generation is beginning to recognize Dufy as a master who could accomplish with pen or brush what lesser craftsmen should never have attempted. We can now discern that his work is so deeply imbued with music that what in the hands of a minor artist remains a child's helicopter is given real wings by his genius to soar in the sky.

Dufy, who has adorned and embellished our existence with thousands of life-enhancing pictures, and whose fertile imagination and extraordinary skill raised the aesthetic level of many industrial products, was one of those artists who develop slowly but then manage to retain their vigorous originality to the very end. Undoubtedly, much of what Dufy produced between c. 1897, the date of his first surviving oil, and c. 1920 is remarkably good, but it is not typically his own. In those years he went through an Impressionist period, became one of the lesser Fauves (the "Wild Beasts," led by Henri Matisse) and briefly subjected himself to both Cézanne's structural harshness and to the theories of the Cubists. Dufy was past forty when he began to realize that he was not meant to be a follower, but had the endowment and discipline to become an originator of charm, wit, fantasy and pleasure. The inimitable (though often clumsily counterfeited) style that he subsequently developed has, indeed, become known as "Dufyesque."

The period between the two world wars, during which his reputation rose to considerable heights, might very well have been called the "Dufy Years." Yet its style has been termed Art Deco (from the word "decorative") and also *Style Poiret,* after Paul Poiret, the *grand couturier* who clothed the ladies of the flaming twenties. It was the world of playboys and playgirls, the age of Cocteau, cocktails and the 1925 International Exhibition of the Decorative Arts in Paris. In all of this Dufy participated. As an employee of Poiret, he contributed to the adornment of well-to-do women. He traveled south in *La Flèche d'Azur* (the Blue Arrow), the crack train connecting Paris and the Riviera, which, in a famous painting, he represented as a diminutive locomotive and five equally toylike cars. In a way, Dufy is the exemplary portrayer of the playgrounds of the triumphant, overstimulated middle class that flooded Paris and the Riviera in the twenties, their dance halls and nightclubs, fast-racing automobiles, the blaring saxophones and pandemonium that not even the Depression and the political upheavals could squelch.

Dufy participated in all of this, but only up to a point. He was sociable, he was gregarious, but he preferred the role of philosophical observer to that of the self-indulgent man-about-town—a preference that allowed him to preserve his sense of values. One is reminded of Watteau who, two centuries earlier, was fascinated by the *fêtes galantes,* but did not take an active part in the frivolity he described. Dufy's pictorial world, like Watteau's, excludes the seamy, the sad, the mad, the tragic, dealing instead with the amusements of the favored few. He recorded the lighthearted aspects and the rippling surfaces of the *haut monde* with sympathy, but often with a trace of melancholy irony. At any rate, it is wrong to confuse the subject matter—admittedly frivolous—with the style, whether we judge an eighteenth-century painter or this master of our time who still lives in the memories of so many dealers, collectors and personal friends.

Raoul Dufy was born on June 3, 1877, at Le Havre, a busy port city on the English Channel. He was the son of the manager of a small metals business who found it hard to support his large family (Raoul had five sisters and three brothers, one of whom, Jean, also became a painter). When the need to earn a living cut short his formal education, he worked as a clerk in a coffee importing firm, but was able to take night classes at the Municipal School of Fine Arts. With a grant allotted him by his native city, he enrolled, after a year's army service, in Léon Bonnat's studio at the Ecole des Beaux-Arts in Paris.

That was in 1900. Nothing spectacular happened to him for the next fifty-three years: he was married to one woman for a long time; he traveled to Munich, Florence, Rome, Sicily, Spain and Morocco; he enjoyed the good things of life, but also worked constantly. At the age of thirty-four, spurred by practical considerations, he joined the establishment of the fashion designer Paul Poiret, who was enthusiastic about Dufy's ideas for textiles. Dufy supplied the designs, engraved the woodblocks and suggested the color schemes, while Poiret made dresses from the fabrics. Subsequently, he was put on salary by the Bianchini silk firm at Lyon. In 1917, he became a curator of the Musée de la Guerre (War Museum) in Paris, where he served until the cessation of hostilities.

His financial situation improved in 1921, after the well-known Galerie Bernheim-Jeune in Paris had given him his first major one-man show. While his paintings began to sell very briskly, Dufy did not spurn occasional commercial jobs: he designed book illustrations, tapestries, ceramics and advertisements, ignoring the absurd distinction between fine and applied arts—an artificial invention of nineteenth-century aesthetics. He agreed with those who believe that it is dangerous to leave art for daily use to unimaginative hacks and that life can be embellished only if good artists participate in the making of utilitarian objects. Dufy's biographer, Jacques Lassaigne, points out that the master's fabrics and hangings reveal "all the skill, taste and aptness with which the innovations of modern painting can be applied to everyday living, to the homes we live in and the clothes we wear."

In the eyes of those who do not consider the birth of every masterpiece an important event, Dufy's life could be judged absolutely uneventful. Nothing interrupted the even course of his existence until he approached seventy; his arthritis became so severe that it seriously hampered the use of his hands and impeded his work. For Renoir, similarly affected forty years earlier, there had been no cure. But Dufy was fortunate enough to benefit by modern medicine and went to Boston, where he was a patient of Dr. Freddie Homburger of the Jewish Memorial Hospital, a pioneer in the treatment of arthritis and himself a painter of sorts. Cortisone therapy allowed him to resume painting and also to travel in the United States. He made many watercolors of the Charles River, Times Square, the Brooklyn Bridge and the Arizona desert. In 1951 he returned to France and settled in Forcalquier, a small town in the south. His final years were full of triumphs. At the Venice Biennale of 1952 he won the first prize for painting. At the Musée d'Art et d'Histoire in Geneva he had his largest exhibition: 114 oils, 56 gouaches and watercolors, 32 drawings, as well as ceramics and book illustrations.

What distinguished him from many a hapless colleague, whose life offers more grist for the Hollywood mills, was an inborn serenity, which kept him from squandering his energies like Gauguin, and a happy temperament, which saved him from the despair of Van Gogh. As one of his biographers put it, "What Van Gogh has done in sorrow, Dufy has done in joy." One of the most versatile artists of his age, he applied his talent in many directions. Behind this drive was his philosophy, not of "art for art's sake," but of "art for life's sake." Once, when asked to explain the role of art in life, he said, "To render beauty accessible to all, by putting order into things and thought."

This emphasis on order is a typically Gallic quality—order, to be understood not as a Prussian propensity for rigid system, but rather as a Latin fondness for clarity of statement, for the logic inherent in form. Form, however, is a creation of the mind which corrects—through simplification, rearrangement and selectivity—the "mistakes" of nature. All of Dufy's drawings and paintings are, to some extent, influenced by physical reality. But what distinguishes his portraits, as well as his landscape paintings, is his insistence upon a reality which the ordinary man does not see.

To achieve his desired effects Dufy had, first, to abandon what was known as correct drawing, and second, to invent a calligraphy of his own. Every canon of the art of picture-making that he had learned at the Ecole des Beaux-Arts as a youth had to be discarded; thus, perspective, when necessary, is sacrificed to the artist's concept of joyous arrangement; chiaroscuro, which the young Dufy had used to create the illusion of space, is rejected for decorative two-dimensionality; and the natural color of an object does not dictate his chromatic choice. With charming spontaneity, the color of an object is allowed to extend far beyond its boundaries.

But we distinguish a genuine Dufy from the work of his countless plagiarists by his draftsmanship, a trait which is as personal as a man's handwriting. His is a sort of cursive stenography composed of little curving strokes that hint at rather than describe, that are light, swift, graceful and seemingly so effortless that they conceal the years of practice and discipline that have gone into them. The virtuosity of Dufy's draftsmanship enhances rather than eclipses the poetry inherent in the things he drew and painted, and its rapidity enabled him to capture moods and movements unrecorded by slower-working painters.

There is a rhythmic quality about his work. After all, Dufy came from a family of music lovers. His father was an amateur musician; one of his brothers became an organist at Le Havre; another, the editor of the *Courrier Musical* in Paris. Orchestras were among the favorite subjects of the artist, and in his pictures he has paid homage to Bach, Mozart and Chopin. In his racetrack fantasies, his gay renderings of Paris, his airy vistas of Nice and Sainte-Adresse, one finds the ordered balance of a Bach fugue, the allegretto rhythm of a Mozart minuet and the debonair dreaminess of a Chopin prelude.

Unlike Utrillo, who painstakingly noted every topographical detail, the places Dufy saw merely served as springboards for his lively imagination. He felt free to "distort" or endow with capricious colors any object that caught his fancy. Accused of taking too many liberties with the motif, the sharp-witted Dufy made one of his famous remarks: "Nature, my dear sir, is only an hypothesis."

All real artists "distort." Between the two world wars, artists indulged in "distortion" either to convey their horror of the organized mass butchery called war and to protest against social injustices, or else to flee from the world of reality entirely, into one of surrealist images. Dufy's purpose was different: he wanted to please, to spread pleasure. The tragic muse was not his. Before Dufy, the French novelist Stendhal had pronounced the rule: "The beautiful is the promise of happiness." Dufy shunned ugliness and intensified the sensuous qualities of the beautiful. The Mediterranean is rarely as phosphorescently blue as on his canvases; flowers, lawns, beaches, palm trees and drawing-room interiors are endowed by his brush with hues so fascinating and infinitely varied that they radiate an optimism that is essential to survival.

If he was not a moralist like Rouault, Dufy was, like his predecessor, a real poet, yet one aware of his limitations. "My eyes were made to erase that which is ugly," he once explained. Gertrude Stein, though she preferred the more powerful, more ardent Picasso, could not resist the subtle effortlessness of the gentler man. "Dufy is pleasure!" she said.

Much of this pleasure came from his chromatics. For all his stupendous dexterity as a draftsman, Dufy was primarily a colorist in the great French tradition of Claude Lorrain, Fragonard, Boucher, Watteau, Delacroix, Manet and Renoir. Like these artists, he used color for the revelation of joy. Those who accused him of catering to the pleasure-seeking upper classes by painting them as they indulged in their expensive entertainments overlooked one fact: that thousands of reproductions of watercolors and oils by Dufy graced, and still grace, the homes of lower middle-class people who never stroll on the green turf of Deauville or on the famous Promenade des Anglais at Nice, and who never take their vacations in Normandy or at Taormina. Millions, all over the world, love his work because Dufy participated in the *comédie humaine,* the *dolce vita,* as an amused spectator who infused his unaggressive wit and humor into everything he painted.

The work he did between 1900 and 1906 is strictly Impressionist in its free and spontaneous reduction of form to spots of color. Yet he paid close attention to design. Moreover, several landscapes suggest that the young man, while still "realistic" in the manner of Monet and Pissarro, may have been exposed to the experiments of the Nabis—Denis, Bonnard, Vuillard and others—who regarded nature as mere raw material to be organized by the artist into a mental image and translated into a composition (for the Nabis, works of art were chiefly metaphors to express feelings).

Dufy's turning point was provided by a visit, late in 1905, to the Salon d'Automne, where he saw Matisse's *Luxe, Calme et Volupté:* "At the sight of this picture I understood the new raison d'être of painting, and Impressionist realism lost its charm for me as I beheld this miracle of creative imagination at play, in color and drawing." But he was not yet ready to plunge into the new stream. *Old Houses at Honfleur* (50) was painted some months after his exposure to the Fauves. The heavy strokes and broad patches of pure color betray the impact made on him by the "cage of the Wild Beasts." The dabs and patches of color, each fully expressive and self-assertive, vary in shape and thickness. By means of bold juxtapositions, these colors take on a great intensity of light that considerably heightens their effect. Yet the Renaissance principles of perspective are still retained, along with other academic features.

The self-liberation took place sometime in 1906. Dufy had grown tired, as he put it years later, of always remaining "outside the picture itself." Setting up his equipment on the beach of Sainte-Adresse, which was to remain one of his favorite sites, he asked himself the crucial question: "How can I use these means [the pigments and brushes] to express not what I see, but what *is,* what exists for me, my reality?" His answer was to blaze a new path for himself: "I had discovered my own system. Its theory is simple. To study sunlight is a waste of time. Light in painting is something quite apart: it is composed, it is arranged, it is colored."

Dufy, thus, had become a real Fauve. But while he would abandon nuances, soft shadings, subtle transitions, along with the traditional perspective, he was destined to be one of the tamest of the Wild Beasts. With ochers and browns he restrained the violence of hot colors; by drawing strong silhouettes he also modified the Fauve rejection of form. He was quite unlike Vlaminck, who painted, in his own words, with "his heart and his guts," without worrying about style. Dufy's aesthetics was much closer to that of Matisse, whose professed goal was to create an "art of balance, of purity and serenity," and who insisted on "conception," on "a clear vision of the whole, right from the start."

Fauvism was spent after two or three years, and virtually all but Matisse replaced their explosions of ultramarine, vermilion, orange and yellow with canvases painted in cooler colors. Joining Braque, another ex-Fauve, at l'Estaque (where Cézanne had produced some of his most important paintings), Dufy, like his colleagues influenced by the Cézanne memorial exhibitions, replaced curved forms with starkly angular ones, made use of muted colors and minimized space recession. Yet he, who had never been able to become a really extreme Fauve, was equally unable to follow Braque further on the road that eventually led to Cubism (Plates 53, 54, and 55 contain some quasi-Cubist features). It was not in his nature to say, like Braque in his Cubist heyday, "The subject is like a fog that has lifted, allowing the objects to appear."

Some of the pictures Dufy produced prior to 1920—that is, before he developed his own, unmistakable Dufyesque style—now often fetch high prices. At a 1969 auction, a Fauve Dufy sold for $140,000. This is due partly to the current interest in Fauvism (the last of the representational schools) and partly to the extreme rarity of Fauve pictures by Dufy. Indeed, early oils by Dufy are not very numerous to begin with.

But around 1920 began the swell of a flood of pictures—oils, watercolors and gouaches—that may run into the thousands. He seems to have found himself again during a prolonged postwar stay at the Riviera hill town of Vence, where his art blossomed into those rococo arrangements of gaily colored curves and arabesques that became his hallmark. His early absorption of Fauvism enabled him to use color as an independent means of expression rather than as a mere complement of design, and to forget all Beaux-Arts dogma about perspective, three-dimensionality and accurate drawing.

There is something refreshingly untutored, even naïve, about the often similar, yet never identical pictures he poured out. In a way, his stick figures, his disklike suns, and his toy cars, trains, boats and steamers are reminiscent of those in paintings by children. Delacroix once praised the ability of "very great men" to keep "part of that impetuosity of their impressions which is characteristic of youth."

Dufy was a hedonist, but one who, instead of selfishly indulging himself, dispensed pleasure to others. And he was also something of a perfectionist. His pictures, seemingly so unpremeditated and spontaneous, are actually the products of one who had full control over his art.

This mastery is worth mentioning in any evaluation of Dufy. In his flower pieces (52, 78), the apparent informality of the blossoms is deceptive; the charmingly casual bouquet in Plate 78 is actually carefully arranged into a spiraling composition that widens as it twists its way up from the plaited base. In his racecourse pictures (56, 72, 89) the scenes are suggested in the sketchiest way; the forms are hardly more than hastily drawn outlines in red, orange or blue, over which the damp brush is quickly run. Thus, the paintings are primarily poems in color rather than accurate descriptions of what a sportsman or spectator sees. The regattas (75, 76) are similarly treated, with the forest of masts, sails and hulls indicated by an interplay of verticals, horizontals and diagonals. Quick broad strokes indicate water and sky, and the figures, their purposeful activity notwithstanding, are suggested more than they are actually delineated.

These examples offer evidence that, after his Realist and Impressionist beginnings, the artist never again engaged in the game of verisimilitude. He was content to abstract essential characteristic forms from the gay scene before him and to arrange them into a strikingly beautiful design that hints at rather than defines. Abstract, too, are his *Orchestra*s. A personal friend of Charles Munch, Dufy regularly attended the rehearsals of the conductor's Paris Conservatory Orchestra, where he made quick preparatory sketches. In these pictures (81), in which the musicians look more like notes on a sheet of music than real people, the weaving patterns of form and sound are superbly translated into vibrating line.

Except for the excruciatingly painful arthritis that plagued his final years, Dufy's long, full life was apparently unmarred by any tragic experiences. At any rate, from his first major one-man show in 1921 to his death thirty-two years later, he enjoyed an unbroken chain of success which he fully deserved. What he stands for in twentieth-century art has been expressed well by Marcel Brion: "Few contemporary artists appear to be so complete, so *accomplished*. Yet in his pictures, one can never detect the smallest sign of labored or painful evolution. Dufy clearly has his place in the French tradition of classical painting."

Courthion, P., *Raoul Dufy,* Paris (1951)
Werner, A., *Dufy,* New York (1953)
Lassaigne, J., *Dufy,* Geneva (1954)
Brion, M., *Dufy,* New York (1958)

LIST OF COLOR PLATES

HENRI ROUSSEAU

48. The Decorated Street, Le Havre. 1906.
49. Sideshow. 1906.
50. Old Houses on the Basin at Honfleur. 1906.
51. The Fourteenth of July at Le Havre. 1906.
52. Amongst the Flowers. 1907.
53. Studio. 1907.
54. Mozart. 1909–1910.
55. Rose in a Room. 1917.
56. Horse Race at Deauville. 1919.
57. Bathing Women. 1920.
58. Sicilian Landscape. 1922.
59. Rowers on the Marne River. 1923.
60. Taormina, The Sea. 1923.
61. View of Sainte-Adresse. 1924.
62. The Beach. 1925.
63. Casino at Nice. 1927.
64. Window Overlooking Nice. 1927.
65. Fountain at Hyères. 1928.
66. Angels' Bay. 1928.
67. Hindu Girl. 1928.
68. Indian Model in the Painter's Studio. 1928.
69. Castle by the Sea. 1928.
70. Paddock. 1930.
71. Portrait of Mme. Dufy. 1930.
72. Races at Ascot. 1931.
73. Portrait of Michael. 1934.
74. Boating. 1935.
75. Deauville Regatta. 1936.
76. Deauville Regatta. 1936.
77. Electricity (detail). 1936–1937.
78. Anemones. 1937.
79. Venice, Piazetta San Marco. 1938.
80. Versailles. c. 1938.
81. Orchestra. c. 1942.
82. Studio with Blue Portfolio. 1942.
83. Moulin de la Galette. 1943.
84. Amphitrite. 1943.
85. Threshing and Binding the Wheat. 1945.
86. The Yellow Console Table. 1947.
87. Homage to Mozart. 1948.
88. The Red Violin. 1948.
89. At Ascot. 1950.
90. The Quintet with the Red Cello. 1948.
91. Mexican Musicians. 1951.
92. The Artist's Studio. 1935–1952.

NOTES ON THE COLOR PLATES

ROUSSEAU (1844–1910). Plates 1–47.

1. *Myself: Portrait-Landscape.* 1890. Oil on canvas. Prague, The Modern Museum. Formally dressed, yet with a cap upon his head, Rousseau stands on one of the Parisian quays, a brush in one hand, and in the other a palette, on which are written the names of his successive wives, Clémence and Joséphine. Though still an unknown at the time, he appears full of confidence. On his lapel he wears a violet button, awarded for his volunteer teaching in a neighborhood school and identifying him as an *officier de l'instruction publique*. Note the flags of many nations on the ship moored at the quay and the row of wine casks outside the customhouse. In the background is the Pont-des-Arts. The balloon and the Eiffel Tower proclaim progress in science and technology.

2. *Carnival Evening.* 1886. Oil on canvas. Philadelphia Museum of Art. This is one of Rousseau's earliest pictures, yet there is nothing amateurish about it. The two young people dressed for a carnival, the bare trees in silhouette with the fretwork of twigs, the mysterious house on the left, the moon and clouds in the dark blue sky, all conjure up a romantic mood, a feeling of strangeness. With great skill, the artist produces in limpid colors the sensation of depth, space and harmony.

3. *Walk in the Forest.* 1886–1890. Oil on canvas. Zurich, Kunsthaus. In terms of its composition, this picture of a fashionably dressed woman waiting on a wooded path is related to Plate 2. Here, as in *Carnival Evening,* the artist has created a real feeling of woods (note the complicated latticework of budding trees) as well as of deep space. A mysterious atmosphere pervades both paintings.

4. *Sunset at Ile Saint-Louis.* 1888. Oil on canvas. Paris, private collec-

tion.   In the foreground is the Ile Saint-Louis, in the heart of Old Paris. On the right, the towers of Notre-Dame can be glimpsed. But the topographical detail of the scene is unimportant. Whatever Rousseau creates has the aura of the unreal, or rather the surreal. The dark shape of a man is barely discernible against the rectangular masses in the foreground (possibly cargo destined for the nearby barge). He and the small figure that casts a long shadow on the deserted quay produce a waiting-for-Godot atmosphere. The ghostliness of the scene is enhanced by the brilliant light of the full moon contrasting with the deep, luminous shadows.

5. *Storm in the Forest*. 1891. Oil on canvas. Radnor, Pennsylvania, Collection Mr. and Mrs. Henry Clifford.   This picture of a tiger about to leap is unsurpassed for its feeling of tension, which extends even to the vegetation, and for its rendering of violent movement. Yet Rousseau never saw tigers in their natural habitat; he observed them only in the Paris Zoo. But he also availed himself of a children's book on animals, whose drawings he zealously copied (the cheap, dog-eared volume that he owned is still preserved). At any rate, Rousseau's imagination was so keen that, through the disposition of his mind, he could summon up any country he wished, complete with its exotic flora and fauna.

6. *The Centenary of Independence*. 1892. Oil on canvas. Düsseldorf, Voemel Collection.   To explain the meaning of this picture, which celebrates the Centenary of the Declaration of Independence, Rousseau wrote for the catalog of the Indépendants' group show: "The people, holding hands, dance round the two Republics, those of 1792 and 1892, to the tune of 'Auprès de ma blonde.' " This tree-circling dance of patriotic peasants in red Phrygian (or "liberty") caps recalls Brueghel's *Wedding Dance in the Open Air* (Detroit Institute of Arts). The fluttering banners are flags of all nations, arranged to stream in the same direction. This jubilant picture is a hymn to freedom. It began as a project for the decoration of a borough hall near Paris.

7. *Sawmill near Paris*. 1890–1893. Oil on canvas. The Art Institute of Chicago.   The composition is unified by the serpentine pattern formed by the road and the piles of timber. At the right a woman carries her child. The boy

24

near her holds a branch, probably cut from the large fruit-bearing tree. Remarkable pictures like these made Rousseau's biographer, Wilhelm Uhde, write: "His passion for work, his willpower, his unshakable confidence set Rousseau apart from ordinary mortals."

8. *Dam.* 1891-1893. Oil on canvas. Paris, private collection. This picture, with its soft blue sky and billowing clouds, the boat, the French flag and, especially, the fishermen, conveys a tranquil Sunday atmosphere. Before the advent of the automobile, fishing was the chief delight of the French *petit-bourgeois:* no body of water was complete without a fisherman. Looking at this picture, with its simplicity and economy of statement, one must agree with Rousseau's self-assessment: "In all my work Sincerity has been observed, and I have always aimed at it in my actions as well as in my work."

9. *The Artillerymen.* c. 1893. Oil on canvas. New York, The Guggenheim Museum. For several years, Rousseau served in the French army. The picture, which conveys memories of his soldiering days, is probably based on a souvenir snapshot. The inscription on the wheel reads: "The fourth battery, the third canon." The soldiers, depicted with wide eyes and identical moustaches, pose stiffly. Regimental swords and guns are planted to the left and right. The undulating landscape echoes the pattern of the figures.

10. *War.* 1894. Oil on canvas. Paris, The Louvre. This picture was preceded by a lithograph on red paper, commissioned by the poet Alfred Jarry for his magazine, *L'Ymagier.* For the catalog of the Salon des Indépendants, Rousseau offered this commentary: "Frightful, she passes, leaving in her wake despair, tears and ruins." The "she" is the strange-looking woman who soars on horseback over a pile of corpses. Brandishing a sword in her right hand and a smoking torch in her left, she is meant to represent evil. Rousseau's sentiments were strongly pacifist.

11. *Portrait of a Young Girl.* 1893–1895. Oil on canvas. The Philadelphia Museum of Art. For this portrait of a proletarian girl from his Plaisance quarter, Rousseau provided a special rural setting and placed sheep—one white, one black—on either side of her in the background. The trees and the

branch she holds are painted with the same imperturbable exactitude as her impassive face, Sunday dress, and fine orange boots.

12. *Path in Parc Montsouris.* 1895. Oil on canvas. New York, private collection. This park is located in the southernmost part of Paris (La Cité Universitaire now borders on it). Deliberately, the artist made the well-trimmed trees loom large. The little figures walking on the gravel path help to fix the bird's-eye perspective.

13. *The Tiger Hunt.* c. 1895. Oil on canvas. The Columbus Gallery of Fine Arts. Like his mentor, Léon Gérôme, Rousseau was fascinated by North African themes. Living in a sordid proletarian neighborhood, which he left infrequently, he loved to withdraw into dream worlds of foreign lands, with the help of newspaper illustrations or postcards. Quietness and lack of motion are expressed in the figures of the Arabs gathered around the dead tiger, the strange hills and the white horse.

14. *Child on the Rocks.* After 1895. Oil on canvas. Washington, D.C., The National Gallery of Art. Rousseau was commissioned to paint this picture in commemoration of a neighborhood child who had just died. The artist was fond of the children of the local tradesmen, and frequently gave them music and drawing lessons. This precocious boy, his inflexible, stout body set off by striped stockings, sits stiffly—as in a late nineteenth-century photograph— yet not uncomfortably amid jagged rocks. His melancholy eyes stare at us with great intensity from beneath heavy brows.

15. *The Quarry.* 1896-1897. Oil on canvas. Private collection. The time is summer, and the vegetation is luxurious. Note the dramatic clouds and the charming details that a more blasé, intellectual artist might have overlooked. But where are the workers in this quarry? Or is this a Sunday scene? The pedestrian may be a painter himself, absorbed in his contemplation of the site. As Roger Shattuck put it, "He found all the scenery he needed in and around Paris" (*The Banquet Years*).

16. *Bouquet of Flowers.* c. 1897. Oil on canvas. Marseilles, private

collection. Rousseau awarded each blossom and leaf equal prominence, painting every detail with minute care. In this respect he differed from the Impressionists, who suppressed details in order to give us the enchantment of misty bouquets and vague atmospheric effects. His approach was also unlike those of such post-Impressionists as Gauguin and Van Gogh, who painted flowers in bold strokes of riotous color. Yet while he assigned the same importance to each blossom and to each leaf, he orchestrated these elements into a unity composed of striking harmonies.

17. *Landscape with Fisherman.* c. 1897. Oil on canvas. Paris, Collection E. Tappenbeck. This is a romantic rendering of one of the countless idyllic and forgotten villages that still existed in prewar France. Save for the smokestack, indicative of the intrusion of modern industrialization, everything here is timeless, old. The trees are stylized, in patterns of playful movement, as elsewhere in Rousseau's work. The artist liked to paint anglers, who typified a pre-industrial innocence.

18. *The Sleeping Gypsy.* 1897. Oil on canvas. New York, The Museum of Modern Art. Daniel Catton Rich called this superbly painted oil "one of the strangest and most moving pictures in all of modern art." This majestic dream image of a huge lion sniffing at the dark-skinned woman is utterly surreal, its unreality enhanced by the addition of the mandolin and the jug. It has been suggested that the lion, as well as the desert landscape, are meant to be projections of the so-called gypsy's dream rather than elements of an actual scene. It has also been pointed out that Rousseau, who ordinarily never forgot realistic details, put no imprints on the sand around the sleeper's feet, as if to say: this is not a real person, only an image in a dream.

19. *Bridge in Paris.* c. 1898. Oil on canvas. Paris, private coll. A boat floats down the Seine. The Eiffel Tower is half-hidden by haze. All objects in this picture—the wood, the houses, the factories—look like neatly wrought toys.

20. *Banks of the Seine.* c. 1898. Oil on canvas. Paris, private collection. Note the delightful way the smoke streams from the large chimney. In an autobiographical sketch Rousseau wrote: "If I have kept my naïveté, it is

because M. Gérôme, who was professor at the Ecoles des Beaux-Arts in Paris and M. Clément, director of the Ecole des Beaux-Arts in Lyon, always told me to do so."

21. *The Tollhouse.* c. 1890. Oil on canvas. London, Courtauld Institute of Art. "Though *The Tollhouse* is worthy of Uccello," André Malraux has written in *The Voices of Silence,* "it is also the landscape of a dream—we need only look at that odd figure posted on a wall." Before World War I, tollhouses like this existed at each of the Paris city gates. The officials there, among them Rousseau, checked the contents of carriages that entered the capital, imposing duty on wine, grain, milk, salt and lamp oil. But here the cityscape has been transformed into a rural scene: the gentle hilly landscape did not exist in reality; it was completely invented.

22. *The Forest of Vincennes.* 1886-1890. Oil on canvas. Basel, private collection. The trees look like dancers in a ballet. Rousseau preferred to paint landscapes in the early spring, when young leaves were unfolding from the branches. This composition of slender bare trunks and, in the background, rich foliage shows a wonderful sense of balance.

23. *Happy Quartet.* 1902. Oil on canvas. New York, Whitney Collection. The naive bucolic scene is also known as *Adam and Eve.* But did the first human pair have a son prior to their departure from Paradise? And what about the domesticated dog? This is probably an allegory of love, with the dog symbolizing fidelity, and is one of Rousseau's few paintings of nudes.

24. *The Mill at Alfort.* c. 1902. Oil on canvas. New York, Collection Mr. and Mrs. E. Josten. "Naïveté is not to be had for the asking. An artist who is asked to be simple ceases to be simple. Rousseau's works have great charm, partly because he did not know he was naive" (*The Language of Painting,* by Charles Johnson, 1943).

25. *Bouquet of Flowers.* 1902-1903. Oil on canvas. London, The Tate Gallery. "The nucleus of the composition consists of dark pansies, whose burnished density is crowned by a light, transparent network of flowers and

leaves radiating around it. The leaves of the pansies are arranged with flawless symmetry; to the yellow flowers on the left corresponds the complementary blue of the flowers on the right; the delicate graphic precision of the plants is set off by the calm uniform tones of white vase, pink background and red rug" (*Still Life Painting,* by Charles Sterling, 1959).

26. *Suburb: Banks of the Marne.* c. 1905. Oil on canvas. Vaduz, Liechtenstein, Collection Dr. Paul Hänggi. Rousseau captures the sparkling atmosphere of a village at the confluence of the Marne and Seine rivers. The red roof accentuates the brightness of the whole painting. Anglers, one of the artist's favorite themes, also appear here.

27. *Child with Puppet.* 1903. Oil on canvas. Winterthur, Switzerland, Kunsthaus. This picture is a commissioned portrait for which the artist received 300 francs, possibly more than any other of his paintings brought him. Rousseau's neighbors often employed the self-taught artist as a portraitist. Carrying a lapful of flowers caught up in his skirt, the child, apparently a boy of about three, dangles a gaily colored marionette, complete with moustache.

28. *Hungry Lion.* 1905. Oil on canvas. Switzerland, private collection. This enormous, mural-like picture, one of a score of paintings by Rousseau that deals with the jungle, was exhibited at the famous Salon d'Automne of 1905 in which Matisse and other innovators participated. In the catalog, Rousseau described his picture: "The hungry lion, throwing himself upon the antelope, devours him; the panther stands by, anxiously waiting for the moment when he can claim his share. Birds of prey have ripped out pieces of flesh from the poor animal who pours forth his death cry! Setting sun."

29. *Country Wedding.* 1905. Oil on canvas. Paris, Collection Mme. Jean Walter. Under a triumphal arch of highly stylized trees, the eight participants pose stiffly and awkwardly, like figures in a daguerreotype. There is little difference in their facial expressions. Yet the grandfather, garbed in a peasant's smock and clutching the text of the speech he is going to make, and the grandmother, who is holding the bride's train, have been endowed with great dignity. Rousseau himself is present: he is standing between mother and sister,

behind the bride. A touching note is provided by the huge black dog who is also an integral part of the family.

30. *Portrait of Pierre Loti.* 1906. Oil on canvas. Zurich, Kunsthaus. Pierre Loti had just published *Au Maroc,* a record of his journey to Fez, and received, at Algiers, the announcement of his recent election to the Académie Française. Hence, he was very much in the news at the time Rousseau painted this picture, after a portrait found in a periodical. Loti, wearing Muhammadan headgear, exhibits a quiet dignity. Both man and animal look at us directly with keen eyes (Loti was a lover of cats, about which he wrote repeatedly). Note the unusual lateral stripes of the cat.

31. *Merry Jesters.* 1906. Oil on canvas. The Philadelphia Museum of Art. In many of Rousseau's jungle scenes, wild beasts are depicted attacking natives or weaker animals. This painting, however, offers a view of silent concord and amity: the creatures pose in complete harmony amidst the unspoiled primordial landscape. But what is the meaning of the inverted milk bottle, spilling its contents? Or of the back scratcher?

32. *Still Life with Coffeepot.* 1907. Oil on canvas. Milan, Collection Gianni Mattioli. In Western art prior to the seventeenth century, still lifes were generally painted as areas of interest within major compositions, rather than as an independent genre. This branch of painting was favored chiefly by artists of the Netherlands and certain of the Spanish painters. In this work, reminiscent of still lifes by Francisco Zurbarán, Rousseau carefully selected and arranged the elements of his subject, giving them an artificial monumentality.

33. *Viaduct at Auteuil.* c. 1907. Oil on canvas. France, private collection. This picture is so meticulously painted that, were it reproduced in black and white, it would resemble an old engraved *veduta.* Everything is firmly handled, with unerring certainty. But while the landscape has a classic appearance, the steamboats, the construction site and the bridge tell us that we are in the twentieth century.

34. *The Snake Charmer.* 1907. Oil on canvas. Paris, The Louvre. An

enigmatic black-skinned woman plays the flute. Intoxicated by the music, snakes stretch, undulate or play around the charmer's neck. Even the water bird is fascinated by the music. The moon quietly looks down on this strange jungle scene. With its contrasts of darkness and wonderfully flowing silvery light, this picture exudes all the mystery of poetry.

35. *Negro Attacked by a Jaguar.* c. 1909. Oil on canvas. Basel, Kunstmuseum. "Few artists have been more jeered at in their lifetime than *le Douanier*" (Guillaume Apollinaire).

36. *The Jungle: Monkeys with Oranges.* 1908. Oil on canvas. New York, private collection. "It was his love of trees that gave rise to his interest in exotic plants" (Dora Vallier). Rousseau sketched these plants in the huge and humid hothouses of the Jardin des Plantes.

37. *Père Juniet's Cart.* 1908. Oil on canvas. Paris, Collection Mme. Jean Walter. Père Juniet was the owner of a grocery in Rousseau's neighborhood. His wife was Rousseau's concierge. She was kind to the aged widower, looking after him and often feeding him. To pay his debt of gratitude, Rousseau made this picture of the family on a Sunday outing in their newly acquired horse and buggy. Rousseau, seated next to Père Juniet, sports a straw hat.

38. *Avenue in the Park of Saint-Cloud.* 1908. Oil on canvas. Frankfurt, Städelsches Institut. The small figures stroll sedately beneath an archway of trees in a park near Paris as though they were walking down the center aisle of a glorious Gothic cathedral. In her book on Rousseau, Dora Vallier has written: "Had Rousseau's name not come down to us, but only his paintings . . . we would refer to him, as we refer to anonymous painters of the past, as 'the Master of the Tree.' No painter has ever been more attracted to foliage, whether stirring tremulously or standing immobile."

39. *View of Malakoff.* 1908. Oil on canvas. Bern, Collection Professor W. Hadhorn. The small study for this picture, rather blurred in an Impressionistic manner, is in the collection of Mrs. Max Weber, widow of Rousseau's disciple, at Great Neck, Long Island. In this final version everything

is precise and distinct: the stonework on the embankment, the porcelain insulators on the poles, the large bows on the women's hats.

40. *Strollers in a Park.* 1907-1908. Oil on canvas. Paris, Collection of Mme. Jean Walter. "There are no amateurs—except those who paint bad pictures" (Edouard Manet).

41. *View of the Pont-de-Sèvres.* 1908. Oil on canvas. Moscow, Pushkin Museum. Originally, the painting included only the balloon. However, Rousseau was so pleased with the new technology that, long after the picture was finished, he added the biplane and the dirigible.

42. *Football Players.* 1908. Oil on canvas. New York, The Guggenheim Museum. The scene in which the action is set—a small clearing in a sunlit autumnal wood—is very strange, indeed. Though the men in the striped suits play football, they seem more like dancers in an avant-garde ballet. Note that the teams are distinguished not only by different uniforms, but also by different hair color. As in other pictures, Rousseau has painted a leaf-by-leaf rendering of the trees. The picture was bought by the Guggenheim Foundation in 1960 at a Sotheby & Co. auction for $103,000, one of the highest prices ever paid for a work by Rousseau.

43. *Vase of Flowers* (second version). 1909. Oil on canvas. Buffalo, Albright-Knox Art Gallery. We can recognize in this picture clusiana, tulip, acacia, daisy, forget-me-not and, in the foreground, a branch of ivy.

44. *The Muse Inspiring the Poet* (first version). 1909. Oil on canvas. Basel, Kunstmuseum. When Rousseau painted this double portrait, the Muse, Marie Laurencin (1885–1956), was actually a very pretty, slim woman in her early twenties, who had just begun to show at the Salon des Indépendants. With her uplifted hand, she makes the gesture of annunciation. The Poet is her lover, Guillaume Apollinaire (1880–1918). Appropriately, he holds a quill in one hand, a scroll in the other. Mlle. Laurencin wears a wreath of pansies.

45. *Landscape with Cow.* c. 1906. Oil on canvas. Paris, private collec-

tion. Though a denizen of Paris for all but the years of his youth, Rousseau had a great yearning for the calm and peacefulness of the countryside. In this bucolic scene, the artist has intentionally exaggerated the size of the cow.

46. *Exotic Landscape.* 1910. Oil on canvas. Washington, D.C., Collection Mrs. Robert R. McCormick. His unfettered fantasy soared to great heights.

47. *Tropical Forest with Monkeys.* 1910. Oil on canvas. New York, Whitney Collection. ". . . a real primitive, a Giotto without training or culture . . ." (Elie Faure).

DUFY (1877–1953). Plates 48–92.

48. *The Decorated Street, Le Havre.* 1906. Oil. Paris, private collection. Throughout Dufy's work, flags appear again and again. Here he depicts a Bastille Day (July 14) celebration in his native city. The large flags seem vastly exaggerated in size compared to the small figures in the street below. Looking down at the street at a forty-five-degree angle, Dufy drew and painted the national flags to create a holiday atmosphere. The flags are suspended in space without any visible support, but this lack of realism does not disturb us.

49. *Sideshow.* 1906. Oil. Zurich, private collection. The gregarious Dufy, a frequent guest at social gatherings, loved people—whether they belonged to the moneyed classes or were ordinary citizens, as is this group gathered in front of a gaudy entertainment booth. He frequently painted street scenes of Paris, where he had moved permanently in 1900. He worked first in the manner of the Impressionists, then, from about 1906 onward, in that of the Fauves (the Wild Beasts). Small details, as well as traditional modeling through light and shadow are omitted. Note the strong black contours around the figures and objects.

50. *Old Houses on the Basin at Honfleur.* 1906. Oil. Paris, Collection Dr. A. Roudinesco. This picture is still closely linked to classical tradition—

houses, pier, boats and water at Honfleur (a port at the mouth of the Seine River) are painted realistically, without any distortion or exaggeration of perspective or size. A black-and-white reproduction might persuade us to categorize this picture as an Impressionist painting. The strong, "unnatural" reds and yellows, however, arbitrarily applied by the young artist for emotional effect, distinguish Dufy's work from that of his predecessors. Dufy had abandoned the Renaissance notion that painting was "imitation of nature."

51. *The Fourteenth of July at Le Havre.* 1906. Oil. Paris, Collection Mme. Bourdon. This picture presents the same subject as *The Decorated Street* (48). But here the flags are much smaller and the people more prominent. Note how the face, in the lower left corner, consists of nothing but a brownish shape divided by a dab of yellow. Although Dufy possessed solid classical training, he often disdained literal, descriptive realism and preferred to render the essence of a scene by focusing on a few general forms and prominent colors.

52. *Amongst the Flowers.* 1907. Oil. Paris, private collection. Nearly all the Impressionists and post-Impressionists liked to paint flowers. Among the Fauves, Dufy and Vlaminck were particularly fascinated by the subject. This is one of Dufy's earliest flower pieces. Though the designs are schematized and abbreviated, botanists have no difficulties in putting each of these flowers in the proper Linnaean category.

53. *Studio.* 1907. Oil. Milan, private collection. This very bold composition was influenced by pre-Cubist tendencies of Dufy's friend Georges Braque. The perspective is purely artificial, ignoring traditional dicta according to which all parallel lines going in one direction meet at a vanishing point. Note the angularity of forms, set off by the nude, whose curves are echoed in the beach chair.

54. *Mozart.* 1909-1910. Oil. New York, Collection Mr. and Mrs. Charles Zadok. An amateur violinist, Dufy shared a love for music with his family: his father was an enthusiastic amateur organist, and two of his brothers were professional musicians. He counted among his close friends the conductor

Charles Munch and the cellist Pablo Casals. Near the base of the Mozart bust can be seen the first four letters of the composer's name. Beneath its apparent spontaneity, Dufy's work is, in its lightness, gaiety and precision, reminiscent of that of *The Magic Flute*'s creator.

55. *Rose in a Room.* 1917. Oil. Paris, Collection Mme. Mathilde Amos. This picture has the buoyancy and cheerfulness of a Mozart minuet. Though small in size, the rose, placed precisely in the center, is the focal point and attracts our total attention. Dufy had no favorite flower—he loved and painted them all. Here he pays homage to the queen of flowers.

56. *Horse Race at Deauville.* 1919. Oil. Dufy is said to have discovered the theme of horse racing when his employer, the silk-manufacturer Bianchini, advised him to attend the races in order to see what women were wearing. But Dufy had eyes only for the jockeys and horses dashing over long stretches of soft green. This picture looks like a quick sketch; yet it is complete and final, conveying the enchanting essence of the scene.

57. *Bathing Women.* 1920. Watercolor and gouache on paper. Formerly Girardin Collection, Paris. As a rule, Dufy liked his models to be of a plump seductiveness. Here, as elsewhere, he makes no attempt to render the psychology of his sitters. In fact, the faces of the three women are almost interchangeable.

58. *Sicilian Landscape.* 1922. Oil. New York, Collection Mr. and Mrs. Charles Zadok. Originally a follower of the Impressionists, Dufy eventually came to resent and deplore their slavish imitation of nature. Although this picture was undoubtedly inspired by what the artist saw and experienced on a Sicilian journey, he managed to weave all of the exotic elements into the pattern of a fairy-tale tapestry.

59. *Rowers on the Marne River.* 1923. Oil. Paris, Collection of Dr. A. Roudinesco. Boating was a favorite theme of such Impressionists as Manet, Monet and Renoir. But while these masters were mainly interested in the interplay of light and air, the less scientific-minded Dufy looked at the world

with the fresh eyes of a child, rendering each aspect of it with equal fascination.

60. *Taormina, The Sea.* 1923. Oil. Paris, Galerie Mouradian-Vallotton. Taormina, Italy's most famous holiday resort, was built on the ruins of ancient Tauromenium. Here, the remains of the large Roman theatre is seen against the blue of sea and sky. The view is breathtakingly beautiful.

61. *View of Sainte-Adresse.* 1924. Oil. Basel, Kunstmuseum. Before he became a Fauve, Dufy often painted Sainte-Adresse, a seaside resort a few miles northwest of Le Havre. These early works are faithful to the actual topography. In the 1920's, when this picture was painted, he merely abstracted from the gay scene a few essential characteristic forms and arranged them in a beautiful design.

62. *The Beach.* 1925. Oil. Solothurn, Switzerland. Collection S. Kocher. This picture exudes all the innocent frolic and merrymaking of the French middle class during the flaming twenties. The bathers' unselfconscious spontaneity is captured in this rendering of a pleasant summer day at the shore.

63. *Casino at Nice.* 1927. Oil. Geneva, Collection of Georges Moos. This large casino, a gambling place destroyed in World War II and never rebuilt, was often painted by Dufy, who liked its bizarre features. The towering palm trees enhance the exotic ambience of the setting.

64. *Window Overlooking Nice.* 1927. Oil. Los Angeles, private collection. The window opens on the broad and elegant Promenade des Anglais which borders part of the bay. Dufy shares with Henri Matisse a predilection for vistas seen through windows.

65. *Fountain at Hyères.* 1928. Oil. Paris, Galerie Louis Carré. Hyères offers quiet, romantic views like this one, seen through the poetic eyes of Dufy, who was fascinated by the fountain's elegance.

66. *Angels' Bay*. 1928. Oil. United States, private collection. Nice, the queen of the Riviera, stretches along the shore of Angels' Bay, well protected by a semicircle of hills. In Dufy's picture, the city and its surroundings seem a playground tailor-made for all the pleasures of the rich.

67. *Hindu Girl*. 1928. Oil. Paris, Galerie Louis Carré. Dufy's nudes are usually too plump and coarse to be attractive. An exception is this painting of the sloe-eyed, voluptuous Anmaviti Pontry. Note the decorative charm of the gay background and the precious traditional sari on which the model is resting.

68. *Indian Model in the Painter's Studio*. 1928. Oil. Paris, Collection M. A. D. Mouradian. From 1911 to his death forty-two years later, Dufy kept the same studio in the Impasse de Guelma, in the heart of Montmartre, near Place Pigalle. Anmaviti Pontry, the Hindu girl of Plate 67, here poses in her colorful sari. The four oriental rugs accent the sitter's exotic quality.

69. *Castle by the Sea*. 1928. Oil. Basel, private collection. Apparently the artist was inspired by a particular, but unidentified, castle in southern France. This picture is so much a fantasy of rich color that its topographical source is uncertain and irrelevant.

70. *Paddock*. 1930. Oil. Zurich, Collection Walter Bär-Halperine. In the paddock, a turf enclosure near the track, the horses are assembled before the race. In the background, the many doors of the stables can be seen.

71. *Portrait of Mme. Dufy*. 1930. Oil. Nice, Musée Masséna. Mme. Dufy appears to have been a chic, patient, self-contained woman. Here, emphasis is given to her expressive hands, which delicately touch her cheeks. The flat blue background is the color of the artist's Impasse de Guelma studio.

72. *Races at Ascot*. 1931. Oil. Paris, Collection Dr. A. Roudinesco. Ascot is to England what Deauville and Longchamps are to France. Watching the races at Ascot, Dufy noted the excitement of the horses and the enthusiasm of the spectators. Later, in his studio, his calligraphic brush recalled the

dynamic scene. Horses and riders, as well as the aficionados on the left, are defined by the barest of outlines.

73. *Portrait of Michael.* 1934. Oil. Paris, Bignou Collection. Michael is a son of the well-known Parisian art dealer, Etienne Bignou. In his youth, Dufy portrayed both himself and members of his family. Later in life, he made very few portraits.

74. *Boating.* 1935. Oil. Los Angeles, private collection. The mood of this picture corresponds to that of Plate 59. Until World War II, boating was a favorite pastime in France. In this soft, dreamy picture, the colors are chosen for their emotionally evocative qualities.

75. *Deauville Regatta.* 1936. Oil. Paris, private collection. A nineteenth-century artist like Monet would have painstakingly depicted sky and sea, embankments and, above all, the reflections of sails and hulls on the shimmering water. Dufy was mainly interested in the interplay of verticals, horizontals and diagonals. Quick broad strokes serve to indicate water and sky.

76. *Deauville Regatta.* 1936. Oil. Paris, private collection.

77. *Electricity* (detail). 1936-1937. Oil. Musée Nationale de la Ville de Paris. Dufy's enormous mural dealing with the history of electricity was executed for the Paris Electrical Supply Company's pavilion at the International Exhibition of Paris, 1937. At the top, Greek deities can be seen; the men on the lower left and right are famous scientists and engineers; the center is a powerhouse with dynamos.

78. *Anemones.* 1937. Watercolor and gouache. Private collection. See Note 52.

79. *Venice, Piazetta San Marco.* 1938. Oil. Paris, Galerie Louis Carré. No other city has been painted as often as Venice. Modern artists who have paid tribute to her evanescent beauty include Monet, Renoir, Signac and Kokoschka. In this charming, light picture the Doge's Palace is seen on the left.

80. *Versailles.* c. 1938. Watercolor. Aquarelle is the most elusive and, therefore, the most demanding of all media. It calls for the utmost spontaneity of vision and speed of execution. Here is a view of the entrance of the Palace of Versailles, the famous residence of King Louis XIV.

81. *Orchestra.* c. 1942. Oil. Paris, Galerie Paul Pétridès. Dufy often attended the rehearsals of the Paris Conservatory Orchestra, whose conductor, Charles Munch, was his close friend. Here, the artist has translated the vigorous movements of the players and the weaving patterns of form and sound into vibrating lines.

82. *Studio with Blue Portfolio.* 1942. Oil. Paris, Galerie Louis Carré. For a change, Dufy has depicted the color of his studio walls in sunny yellow instead of the usual blue. Since an atelier is where an artist spends most of his time, he is likely to render it with great tenderness. The sketch of the violin, an instrument the artist himself played, and the marble statue serve as a substitute for the human presence.

83. *Moulin de la Galette.* 1943. Oil. Paris, Galerie Louis Carré. This work is a free version of Renoir's celebrated painting of 1876. While Dufy closely adheres to the composition of the Impressionist master, his quick, agitated treatment of the theme is lighter and more elusive.

84. *Amphitrite.* 1943. Oil. Formerly Collection Mme. Raoul Dufy, Paris. According to ancient Greek mythology, Amphitrite, daughter of Nereus and wife of Poseidon, was a sea-goddess. But Dufy was not interested in her legendary significance. Instead, he used the mythological title for his rendering of a plump nude, seated on a beach towel and holding a shell in her right hand.

85. *Threshing and Binding the Wheat.* 1945. Oil. Paris, Collection Louis Carré. Harvest scenes have been painted by Brueghel and in recent times by Monet, Gauguin, Van Gogh and Vlaminck. Though he spent most of his time in large cities, Dufy was fond of the French countryside, its wheatfields, and its scenes of agricultural labor.

86. *The Yellow Console Table.* 1947. Oil. Paris, Galerie Louis Carré. This Louis XIV table, which stood in Dufy's studio, appears in many of his drawings and paintings.

87. *Homage to Mozart.* 1948. Oil. New York, Collection of Diane Esmond. This picture, related in subject to Plate 54, suggests an allegretto by Mozart, whose rococo spirit, aristocratic and refined, was very much akin to that of the modern painter.

88. *The Red Violin.* 1948. Oil. Paris, private collection. The table on which the violin rests is rendered with the utmost economy and simplicity. Nowhere is Dufy as abstract as in this picture.

89. *At Ascot.* 1950. Oil. The locale is the same as in Plate 72, *Races at Ascot,* but here no race is being run. Jockeys exercise their horses, while the sportsmen and their elegantly dressed ladies casually stroll around the paddock.

90. *The Quintet with the Red Cello.* 1948. Oil. Paris, private collection. The cellist Pablo Casals once remarked that Dufy's pictorial interpretation of music was so subtle that he (Casals) could tell in what key a particular piece was written, even if he could not guess which piece the musicians were playing.

91. *Mexican Musicians.* 1951. Oil. Formerly Collection Mme. Raoul Dufy, Paris. Groups of minstrels, called *mariachis,* wander throughout much of Mexico. Dressed in their traditional *charro* costume, these musicians play guitars and fiddles as an accompaniment to their fine voices.

92. *The Artist's Studio.* 1935–1952. Oil. Paris, private collection. This picture, begun in 1935, was not finished until 1952. Dufy's Montmartre studio, though empty, breathes an atmosphere of intimacy. The perspective, with its downward thrust on the right and its upward focus on the left, pointing to the doorway and the room beyond, keeps the viewer's eye engaged in movement.

THE PLATES

1
Rousseau: *Myself: Portrait-Landscape.* 1890. Oil on canvas. 56 × 43½ in. Prague, The Modern Museum. The picture has the grandeur of a Renaissance portrait.

2 Rousseau: *Carnival Evening*. 1886. Oil on canvas. 43⅞ × 34¼ in. Philadelphia Museum of Art. The branches and twigs are rendered like delicate nerves.

3   Rousseau: *Walk in the Forest*.   1886–1890.   Oil on canvas.   28 × 23⅝ in.   Zurich, Kunsthaus. Among his coevals, only Odilon Redon's work shares Rousseau's dreamlike quality.

4 Rousseau: *Sunset at Ile Saint-Louis*. 1888. Oil on canvas. 18⅛ × 21¾ in. Paris, private collection. Rousseau's pictures are often provocatively mysterious.

5   Rousseau: *Storm in the Forest*. 1891. Oil on canvas. 51 × 63 in. Radnor, Pennsylvania, Collection Mr. and Mrs. Henry Clifford. The jungle later became a favorite theme of Rousseau's.

6   Rousseau: *The Centenary of Independence*. 1892. Oil on canvas. 44 × 61⅞ in. Düsseldorf, Voemel Collection. The group standing at the right is clad in eighteenth-century costume.

7 Rousseau: *Sawmill near Paris*. 1890–1893. Oil on canvas. 10 × 17¾ in. The Art Institute of Chicago. Psychiatrists consider Rousseau a child-man, with the mentality of a boy of six.

8　Rousseau: *Dam*.　1891–1893.　Oil on canvas.　14¼ × 18⅞ in.　Paris, private collection.　The poet Guillaume Apollinaire insisted that Rousseau must not change his manner of painting.

9 Rousseau: *The Artillerymen*. c. 1893. Oil on canvas. 28¼ × 35⅜ in. New York, The Guggenheim Museum. "Rousseau saw the world with the eyes of a child" (Fernande Olivier).

10 Rousseau: *War*. 1894. Oil on canvas. 44⅜ × 76 in. Paris, The Louvre. A print of popular origin, *The Battle of the Pyramids,* inspired this painting.

11 Rousseau: *Portrait of a Young Girl*. 1893–1895. Oil on canvas. 24 × 17⅞ in. The Philadelphia Museum of Art.

12
Rousseau: *Path in Parc Montsouris*. 1895. Oil on canvas. 29¾ × 18½ in. New York, private collection. His vision was untrammeled, and he took nothing for granted.

13   Rousseau: *The Tiger Hunt.*   c.   1895.   Oil on canvas.   15 × 18⅛ in.   The Columbus Gallery of Fine Arts.   His canvases were greeted with jeers at the Salon des Indépendants.

14 Rousseau: *Child on the Rocks*. After 1895. Oil on canvas. 21½ × 17½ in. Washington, D.C., The National Gallery of Art. Some of Picasso's portraits of children recall Rousseau's.

15 Rousseau: *The Quarry*. 1896–1897. Oil on canvas. 18¾ × 21¾ in. Private collection.
Rousseau had a highly developed sense of color values.

←16 Rousseau: *Bouquet of Flowers.* c. 1897. Oil on canvas. 12⅞ × 9¾ in. Marseilles, private collection. Paul Klee was an ardent admirer of Rousseau.

17 Rousseau: *Landscape with Fisherman.* c. 1897. Oil on canvas. 9¼ × 14⅝ in. Paris, Collection E. Tappenbeck. Here is the poetry of a folk artist of uninhibited expressiveness.

18
Rousseau: *The Sleeping Gypsy*. 1897. Oil on canvas. 51 × 79 in. New York, The Museum of Modern Art. The moon has been given a face.

19 Rousseau: *Bridge in Paris.* c. 1898. Oil on canvas. 12⅞ × 18⅛ in. Paris, private collection. The picture demonstrates the artist's great technical competence.

20 Rousseau: *Banks of the Seine.* c. 1898. Oil on canvas. 12¾ × 15¾ in. Paris, private collection. "An artist of undeniable authenticity" (André Salmon).

←21 Rousseau: *The Tollhouse*. c. 1890. Oil on canvas. 15⅝ × 12⅞ in. London, Courtauld Institute of Art. Green, in countless nuances, dominates this canvas.

22 Rousseau: *The Forest of Vincennes*. 1886–1890. Oil on canvas. 18⅛ × 21⅝ in. Basel, private collection. Rousseau's artistic gift was a phenomenon beyond rational explanation.

23
Rousseau: *Happy Quartet*. 1902. Oil on canvas. 37 × 22½ in. New York, The Whitney Collection. His true talent is revealed as a teller of fairy tales.

24 Rousseau: *The Mill at Alfort.*   c. 1902.   Oil on canvas.   14¾ × 17⅝ in.   New York, Collection Mr. and Mrs. E. Josten.   A sketchier version of this painting is in a Paris collection.

25   Rousseau: *Bouquet of Flowers*.   1902–1903.   Oil on canvas. 24 × 19½ in.   London, The Tate
Gallery.   Very few flower pieces by Rousseau are extant.

26 Rousseau: *Suburb: Banks of the Marne.* c. 1905. Oil on canvas. 18¾ × 25¼ in. Vaduz, Liechtenstein, Collection Dr. Paul Hänggi.

←27   Rousseau: *Child with Puppet.* 1903. Oil on canvas. 39⅜ × 31⅞ in. Winterthur, Switzerland, Kunsthaus. Neighbors had their children "photographed" by Rousseau.

28   Rousseau: *Hungry Lion.* 1905. Oil on canvas. 78¾ × 118⅛ in. Switzerland, private collection. Note the bloody gashes in the antelope's body.

29   Rousseau: *Country Wedding*.   1905.   Oil on canvas.   63¾ × 44½ in.   Paris, Collection Mme.
Jean Walter.   This painting is among Rousseau's largest canvases.

30 Rousseau: *Portrait of Pierre Loti*. 1906. Oil on canvas. 24 × 19⅝ in. Zurich, Kunsthaus.
The writer Georges Courteline kept this portrait in his collection of funny pictures.

31   Rousseau: *Merry Jesters*. 1906. Oil on canvas. 57 × 44 in. The Philadelphia Museum of Art. A work the lawyer Guilhermet produced in court to demonstrate his client's imbecility.

32　Rousseau: *Still Life with Coffeepot.* 1907. Oil on canvas.　15 × 18⅛ in.　Milan, Collection Gianni Mattioli.　Rousseau painted still lifes not for Salon exhibitions, but for pleasure.

33 Rousseau: *Viaduct at Auteuil*. c. 1907. Oil on canvas. 33½ × 45½ in. France, private collection. Rousseau considered himself "one of our best realist painters."

34 Rousseau: *The Snake Charmer*. 1907. Oil on canvas. 65 × 73¼ in. Paris, The Louvre. This picture was commissioned by the mother of the painter Robert Delaunay.

35   Rousseau: *Negro Attacked by a Jaguar.* c. 1909.   Oil on canvas.   44⅛ × 66⅛ in.   Basel, Kunstmuseum.   The picture-book source of this painting shows a keeper playing with a jaguar.

36 Rousseau: *The Jungle: Monkeys with Oranges.* 1908. Oil on canvas. 45¼ × 34⅞ in. New York, private collection.

37 Rousseau: *Père Juniet's Cart*. 1908. Oil on canvas. 38⅛ × 50¾ in. Paris, Collection Mme. Jean Walter. This is the same family that is represented in *Country Wedding* (Plate 29).

38 Rousseau: *Avenue in the Park of Saint-Cloud.* 1908. Oil on canvas. 25 × 14⅝ in. Frankfurt, Städelsches Institut. Here Rousseau returns to an earlier theme (see Plate 12).

39 Rousseau: *View of Malakoff*. 1908. Oil on canvas. 16½ × 21⅝ in. Bern, Collection Professor W. Hadhorn. Rousseau's work repudiates the tyranny of academic art.

40 Rousseau: *Strollers in a Park*. 1907–1908. Oil on canvas. 21⅝ × 18⅛ in. Paris, Collection Mme. Jean Walter.

41 Rousseau: *View of the Pont-de-Sèvres*. 1908. Oil on canvas. 31½ × 40⅛ in. Moscow, Pushkin Museum. In his own words, Rousseau aspired to "the Beautiful and the Good."

42   Rousseau: *Football Players.*   1908.   Oil on canvas.   39⅜ × 31½ in.   New York, The Guggenheim Museum.   Note that the players cast no shadows.

43   Rousseau: *Vase of Flowers*.   1909.   Oil on canvas.   18½ × 13¼ in.   Buffalo, Albright-Knox
Art Gallery.   A late witness to Rousseau's lasting love of flowers.

44 Rousseau: *The Muse Inspiring the Poet.* 1909. Oil on canvas. 57½ × 38⅛ in. Basel, Kunstmuseum. Rousseau took measurements of the sitters with a tailor's tape.

45   Rousseau: *Landscape with Cow*. c. 1906. Oil on canvas.   13 × 18⅛ in.   Paris, private collection.   Note the monumental size of the animal.

46 Rousseau: *Exotic Landscape*. 1910. Oil on canvas. 50¾ × 63¾ in. Washington, D.C., Collection Mrs. Robert R. McCormick.   The active life and the contemplative life in the jungle.

47   Rousseau: *Tropical Forest with Monkeys.* **1910.   Oil on canvas.   50¾ × 62⅞ in.   New York, Whitney Collection.   Rousseau was preoccupied with jungle subjects until the very end.**

48 Dufy: *The Decorated Street, Le Havre.* 1906. Oil. 31⅞ × 25⅝ in. Paris, private collection. Before Dufy, Manet, Monet and Van Gogh had also loved to paint flag-draped streets.

49 Dufy: *Sideshow*. 1906. Oil. Zurich, private collection. An informal gathering of people at a street carnival, seen through the eyes of an initiate to Fauvism.

50 Dufy: *Old Houses on the Basin at Honfleur.* 1906. Oil. 23⅝ × 28¾ in. Paris, Collection Dr. A. Roudinesco. Honfleur was favored by painters of romantic scenes.

51   Dufy: *The Fourteenth of July at Le Havre*.   1906.   Oil.   18 × 15 in.   Paris, Collection Mme. Bourdon.   Dufy's Bastille Day paintings were inspired by aesthetics, not patriotism.

52 Dufy. *Amongst the Flowers.* 1907. Oil. 35⅜ × 30⅜ in. Paris, private collection. Dufy has painted the girl's head as if she, too, were a flower.

53 Dufy: *Studio*. 1907. Oil. 21⅞ × 18¼ in. Milàn, private collection. The picture is divided into several large fields of almost uniformly flat color.

54 Dufy: *Mozart*. 1909–1910. Oil. 18⅛ × 15 in. New York, Collection Mr. and Mrs. Charles Zadok. Note vestiges of Cubist influence in the upper half of the canvas.

55   Dufy: *Rose in a Room*. 1917. Oil. 45¼ × 35½ in. Paris, Collection Mme. Mathilde Amos. Note the many subtle tones and shades of green.

56 Dufy: *Horse Race at Deauville*. 1919. Oil. For the past hundred years, Deauville has been the most elegant seaside resort in France.

←57   Dufy: *Bathing Women*. 1920. Watercolor and gouache. 31½ × 22½ in. Formerly Girardin Collection, Paris. This motif appears frequently in Dufy's oeuvre.

58   Dufy: *Sicilian Landscape*. 1922. Oil. New York, Collection Mr. and Mrs. Charles Zadok. This enchanting setting could be the backdrop for an opera or ballet.

59 Dufy: *Rowers on the Marne River*. 1923. Oil. 23⅝ × 28¾ in. Paris, Collection Dr. A. Roudinesco. Note the rhythmic distribution of the brick red accents throughout the picture.

60 Dufy: *Taormina, The Sea*. 1923. Oil. 31⅞ × 39⅜ in. Paris, Galerie Mouradian-Vallotton.
Dufy makes the most of the dramatic contrast between red and blue.

61 Dufy: *View of Sainte-Adresse*. 1924. Oil. 20⅞ × 25½ in. Basel, Kunstmuseum. The English Channel is rarely as blue as in this picture.

62   Dufy: *The Beach*. 1925. Oil. 25⅝ × 31½ in. Solothurn, Switzerland, Collection S. Kocher.
Note the rhythms of the accented parallel strokes, all contributing to the effect of a rich tapestry.

63 Dufy: *Casino at Nice*. 1927. Oil. 20⅛ × 23⅝ in. Geneva, Collection Georges Moos. This scene on the French Riviera resembles a glimpse into the world of *The Arabian Nights*.

64 Dufy: *Window Overlooking Nice*. 1927. Oil. 21⅝ × 18⅛ in. Los Angeles, private collection. The ocean's soft blue, repeated in the mountains on the horizon, integrates the scene.

65 Dufy: *Fountain at Hyères*. 1928. Oil. 31⅞ × 25⅝ in. Paris, Galerie Louis Carré. Bright accents of red—the roofs of houses above the town—crown the picture.

66 Dufy: *Angels' Bay*. 1928. Oil. 23⅝ × 28¾ in. United States, private collection. When Gertrude Stein exclaimed, "Dufy is pleasure!", she must have had pictures like this in mind.

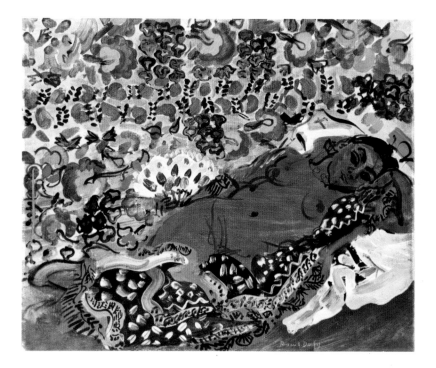

67   Dufy: *Hindu Girl*. 1928. Oil. 18⅛ × 21⅝ in. Paris, Galerie Louis Carré. The woman rests here as if she were an ebony carving set on a luxurious tablecloth.

68 Dufy: *Indian Model in the Painter's Studio*. 1928. Oil. 31⅞ × 39⅜ in. Paris, Collection M. A. D. Mouradian.   In this painting, the setting equals the model in exoticism.

69   Dufy: *Castle by the Sea*. 1928. Oil. 26 × 22 in. Basel, private collection. In the foreground, Dufy defines the subtropical vegetation by curves and arabesques of the brush.

70 Dufy: *Paddock*. 1930. Oil. 17¾ × 21¼ in. Zurich, Collection Walter Bär-Halperine. The horses are painted in purely arbitrary colors, but seem quite natural in their surroundings.

←71   Dufy: *Portrait of Mme. Dufy.*   1930.   Oil.   39⅜ × 31⅞ in.   Nice, Musée Masséna.   Mme. Dufy, who died in 1962, left her collection of her husband's pictures to French museums.

72   Dufy: *Races at Ascot.*   1931.   Oil.   21¼ × 25⅝ in.   Paris, Collection Dr. A. Roudinesco. Note the Union Jack fluttering above the brick red stadium.

73 Dufy: *Portrait of Michael*. 1934. Oil. 31⅞ × 25⅝ in. Paris, Bignou Collection. A very simplified, yet convincing treatment of the sitter's personality.

74 Dufy: *Boating*. 1935. Oil. Los Angeles, private collection. The idyllic quality of this composition seems to be momentarily overcast by a passing cloud.

75 Dufy: *Deauville Regatta*. 1936. Oil. 13 × 31⅞ in. Paris, private collection. Though an oil, this picture conveys the charming sketchiness of a watercolor.

76 Dufy: *Deauville Regatta.* 1936. Oil. 13 × 31⅞ in. Paris, private collection.

77 Dufy: *Electricity* (detail). 1936–1937. Oil. 200 × 35 ft. Musée National de la Ville de Paris. This work is claimed to be the world's largest mural. Only the central portion is shown.

78 Dufy: *Anemones*. 1937. Watercolor and gouache. 25⅝ × 19⅝ in. Private collection. Dufy brings freshness and imagination to a theme which becomes banal in less gifted hands.

79   Dufy: *Venice, Piazetta San Marco.* 1938.   Oil.   20 × 26 in.   Paris, Galerie Louis Carré.   The two carabinieri and a few other scattered figures people the almost deserted square.

80 Dufy: *Versailles.* c. 1938.   Watercolor.   Dufy spent years acquiring his facility as an **aquarel-list**, displayed here in the brilliant simplification of a complex architectural setting.

81 Dufy: *Orchestra.* c. 1942. Oil. 25⅝ × 31⅝ in. Paris, Galerie Paul Pétridès. The subtle shades of red suggest the resonant sound of the music.

82 Dufy: *Studio with Blue Portfolio.* 1942. Oil. 25⅝ × 31⅞ in. Paris, Galerie Louis Carré.
Some of Dufy's own canvases can be seen on the floor and wall.

83 Dufy: *Moulin de la Galette*. 1943. Oil. 51⅛ × 63¾ in. Paris, Galerie Louis Carré. The Moulin de la Galette was a famous dance hall during *La Belle Epoque*.

84 Dufy: *Amphitrite*. 1943. Oil. 94⅜ × 74¾ in. Formerly Collection Mme. Raoul Dufy, Paris. Dufy's blues are always full of mystery.

85 Dufy: *Threshing and Binding the Wheat*. 1945. Oil. 25½ × 31⅞ in. Paris, Collection Louis Carré. The farmers are trying to bring in their grain before the storm breaks.

86 Dufy: *The Yellow Console Table.* 1947. Oil. 39⅜ × 31⅞ in. Paris, Galerie Louis Carré.
In his final years, Dufy often painted pictures dominated by one color.

87 Dufy: *Homage to Mozart.* 1948. Oil. 35 × 45⅝ in. New York, Collection Diane Esmond. Dufy completed this picture despite his constant pain from arthritis.

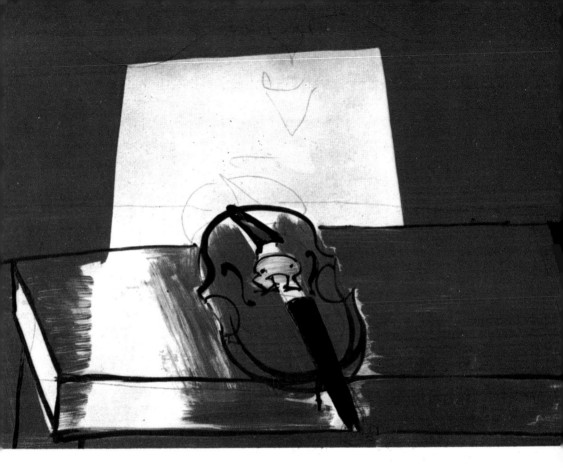

88 Dufy: *The Red Violin*. 1948. Oil. 15 × 20⅛ in. Paris, private collection. The arabesques of the violin contrast sharply with the blank sheet of paper.

89 Dufy: *At Ascot*. 1950. Oil. In his paintings of racing scenes, Dufy continues to explore a theme which had previously fascinated Degas.

90 Dufy: *The Quintet with the Red Cello.* 1948. Oil. 23⅝ × 28¾ in. Paris, private collection. Dufy's spontaneous calligraphic style partakes of the intimacy of chamber music.

91 Dufy: *Mexican Musicians*. 1951. Oil. 31½ × 39⅜ in. Formerly Collection Mme. Raoul Dufy, Paris. One can guess the improvisatory quality of the music from looking at this picture.

92   Dufy: *The Artist's Studio*. 1935–1952. Oil. 35 × 45¾ in. Paris, private collection. The picture above the sofa, at the left, is Dufy's *Red Violin* (Plate 88).